Contents

TITLE PAGE

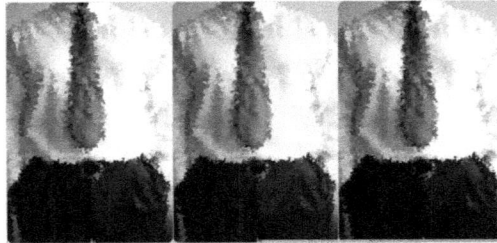

Male Insight

Bridging The Gap

PREFACE

This literature is written with the intent to create a better understanding of men for women. It is written by men for women, about men. It is not a manual that covers all scenarios, as every person is different, and every individual has their own experiences that make them unique. These pages encompass a wealth of knowledge, understanding, and a desire to bridge the gap that promising relationships fall into time and time again.

The goal is to address questions that many women ask about male behavior. Most women tend to want to know the 'WHY' and in response I offer this information. I implore women to read, and challenge prior thinking and perceived notions that have kept men and women from being as close as they could be.

The reader must have an open mind. It is geared for a mature reader and expands in directions different than prior relationships, encounters, knowledge, and beliefs. Information is like love. One can only receive it, if they are open to it fully – no boundaries. It cannot be compartmentalized or re-molded to fit into a 'safe-zone', as the information will then become skewed and misinterpreted…like love.

One's labor for information/love bears no change, no fruit, and no advancement without the ability to adapt.

I will be the first to acknowledge that men have their shortcomings and are a constant work in progress. As you read, remember this is to understand men better and that they (men) will have to do their part to understand women better as well.

Relationships are complicated. Period. There are no two-ways about it. It is an epic consistent show of compassion, humility, courage, patience, and compromise. With all the work that is put into a relationship it is a wonder why we long to be in them. The answer is simple. Love. The hope that someone will love you for who you are, not care about who you were, and fall deeper in love with the person you plan to be. The promise that grows into the bond of forever. There is no greater feeling than that of being loved 'completely'. Hopefully it is that desire that has led you to these pages. Enjoy.

KNOW THY SELF

Chapter 1

If you do not know who you are, how can you know if a man is right for you? Many of you reading will say that you know yourself, but consider the following: As you grow and evolve into the advanced stages of life, the person you were six weeks to six months ago is probably not the same person you are now. To understand a man, any man, as a woman you must know who you are, what you want, where are you going, and how to remain true to yourself.

If someone asked you, "Who are you", and you had to explain who you are without using your name, what would you say? The speech would include a list of accomplishments, accolades, and affiliations, but is that all you, as a woman, are composed of? If so, dig deeper. As a human being it is common to avoid random efforts of soul-searching, but when we do search, how deep do we actually go? The person we come to be is a result of love, pain, morals, accomplishments, failures, and the influence of the people that shape our lives.

Knowing, accepting, and processing this information on a consistent basis is key to how we interact with each other. To know who you are, ask yourself the tough questions, and be brutally honest with yourself. Am I ready to love? Have I dealt with issues from my past? How is my relationship with my parents, and is it affecting me now? Am I ready to trust? Am I open to new things? What is my moral compass? Am I taking self-inventory often enough? What am I willing to sacrifice for my goals in life and love? Am I as emotionally strong as I think I am? What is important to me? Who is important to me? Do I love myself enough or too much? What do I need to improve about who I am? What is happiness to me? Do I know my body? How are my communication skills? Where am I in my faith?

These are just a few questions that one should ask themselves, and ask often. Self-evaluation is a key element to staying in touch with who you are, and who you are becoming. With that in mind, we move forward.

When you meet a man or if you already have one, the subject of 'what do you want' will or should come up. If he does not ask, you may want to evaluate his ability to learn more about you. The subject can only be addressed if you know who you are. (Hence the first topic) Keep in mind that you do not want to limit this topic to bare necessities. As you explore this area alone, you may be forced to go back and ask yourself some additional questions about YOU. Again, be extremely candid with yourself. It is easy to name the materialistic things you desire; and the physical characteristics of the man you want; and the number of kids and pets, but is that all that you want? Take into consideration the prior subject and branch your answers from there.

One of the topics that is consistently overlooked is intimacy. You can only offer instructions or feedback if you have some idea of your own body. Although affection is displayed in many ways do not underestimate the importance of knowing your intimacy needs and desires. This area will change as you continue to mature and enhance your experiences. As you recognize and become comfortable with this evolution, be sure to communicate these changes to your man. If he continues to use what worked three years ago because that is all he knows due to lack of information from you, then you will become frustrated and have only yourself to blame. If you are communicating and he is not listening, then that is another issue.

Now that you know who you are and know what you want, you can begin to figure out 'where you are going.'

Typically where you are going is goal-oriented, driven by the answers to most of the afore mentioned questions. These goals should be consistent to the core of who you are and desire to become. They should not waiver, but only be modified along the way as you execute your plan of action.

Is your list of questions to yourself growing? I hope so. Does it seem like a lot of work? I hope so, and I hope that you feel that you are worth it.

More relationships result in hurt than success, but most of us(men and women) hurt even more due to not having ourselves together prior to being in the next relationship. If you know yourself, you can encounter all that a relationship has to offer openly and honestly. As dynamic as a woman can be, knowing thyself prior to giving of yourself, strengthens you more than you can imagine. Own that strength and lean on it in times of need.

You are probably wondering how is it you have come here to read about men and their tendencies, but are now looking internally. Well, as with the search for ANY truth, it begins within. Let's move forward.

MEETING MEN

Chapter 2

It is evident by the number of wasted, meaningless, bitter relationship endings that there are some mismanaged dialogues from when men and women cross paths. In addition to weeding out the conniving lying man, women need to also weed out men that are not a good match for them. This goes back to knowing yourself first. If a woman is just dating to be dating and having fun, the following may not apply.

First decide that you are ready to date, and subsequently will be emotionally available to be in a relationship should things progress. This means that there has been ample time to heal from a prior relationship, you are not 'just lonely', nor are you carrying an unmanageable amount of personal baggage. The key term is 'unmanageable', as we all have and will continue to have some level of baggage in life.

In attempting to meet a man, and to move towards a relationship, it is common to take the easy way out. It is very rare that the club scene produces meaningful relationships, considering that the energy and environment has blinded most patrons with short term goals. A bar falls in the same category, as alcohol tends to impair most people's judgment, thus you are meeting the inner animal of whoever approaches. Liquid courage can make the average man into a tiger upon approach, but he may only be a tiger cub the next day.

It is always productive to involve yourself in social activities that are of your interest. Participating in these events it offers a dual benefit. You are doing something that you enjoy, and if you meet someone while engaging in these events, you know you have something in common. You can build upon this common ground conversation-wise once a mutual interest is shown.

Prior to heading out into the realm of the dating world, I would suggest that you make two lists.

The first list is the *Hierarchy of Ten*. This is the rank of what is important in a relationship to you. As you grow and expand some of the items on this list may change by going up or down in level of importance. Store this list away, and reference it from time to time to ensure it is a solid depiction of you. Ultimately, you hope that the man you select long term has a Hierarchy of Ten that is similar to yours.

The second list is your *Deal Breaker Ten*. This is the list of ten things that are 'stop signs' for the men you encounter. The items that you know are not conducive to a good relationship for YOU. These are meaningful items. Children, healthy lifestyle, financial responsibility, are all possible examples of what could make this list. Height, skin complexion, net worth, are NOT items for this list due to being superficial. The Deal Breaker Ten is the starting point from which your Core Questions (covered shortly) are derived from.

If you desire a family at some point, there is no point in dating a man who has no desire to have children for six months before finding out. Refer to your Deal Breaker Ten often to ensure that all aspects are covered before investing too much time and energy.

So you have met someone that you think you like? This is typically the area where both men and women go wrong. Neither party wants to be too forward in getting to know each other, so there are a considerable amount of assumptions and misplaced expectations. It is okay to offer the most pleasant disposition at the initial meeting, but if time permits for conversation to move towards direct dialogue that offers a simple yes or no…then do so. This is a chance to cover some of your Core Questions. If the encounter is brief, ensure that as the interaction and dialogue increases, direct conversation is instituted to avoid wasting each others time. The time for high school dialogue is over, so be mature in your fact finding. I am not implying a machine gun version of questioning, but it is apparent that many of us are not asking the appropriate questions to be able to recognize potential relationship hazards. Using your feelings to guide your way through can impair your better judgment.

Your *Core Questions*, when meeting a man, should secure information to determine compatibility.

If you have children, you should ask, if he likes-enjoys-wants children in his life. If he does not want children or does not present himself as 'kid-friendly', this is an issue that can not be avoided. If you have two children and do not plan on having anymore, but he has none and/or desires a big family; an understanding needs to be met or a decision has to be made. This is an issue that is commonly overlooked, and can emotionally bond you to a man who only has the potential to be a short term partner.

Discuss his career goals, and where he sees himself in three years. An aspiring doctor or lawyer sounds great in conversation, but the reality is that both professions are initially very time consuming and require great attention to detail. The woman selected by this man cannot garnish major amounts of his time and attention. She has to be self-sustained, patient, and very understanding. So process the information he shares accurately and with considerable thought.

Inquire about his views on life. If he is just living in the moment and for the here and now, then his spontaneity may be a plus. On the other hand, if you desire someone a little more consistent and stable, he may not be the man for you. If he answers in a way to confirm that he is an extremely focused and driven individual, that information is essential. His personal priorities may outweigh the early stages of a relationship at any given point in time, and you have to be ready for that.

In general conversation if he says he is not looking for anything serious right now or he is just dating; take that at 'face value.' Avoid attempts to consciously wear him down, or sleep with him in order to be next in line for a relationship when that time comes. Men are not built that way.

As you weave your way through a maze of men, you may find that some could be great friends and others may be potential men of interest. Avoid becoming an 'over-looker' or a 'potential-patty."

An '*Over-looker*' becomes so pressed at the prospect of a man that she overlooks items that would appear on her Deal Breaker Ten, which are possessed by the man she is interested in.

Example: A man has a close relationship with his mother who is very supportive and caters to his every whim. His mother washes his clothes, cooks meals for him, and even cleans up after him. The man states that he wants a woman like his mother. An 'Over-looker' will fail to recognize the fact that she is not built that way, and attempts to become that woman in efforts to secure that man. She will make every effort possible, only to lose her own identity or become frustrated with the relationship and leave. Either of the endings results in a broken soul-of-a-woman and time lost.

A '*Potential-Patty*' makes her decision based not on what the man is now, but what SHE views his potential to be. In her mind she sees the future habits, physical likeness, and career path for him, and none of this is based on what HE has shared his goals to be.

Example: A man has a promising career at a marketing firm. His corporate career is funding his musical aspirations of being a professional Bass player. And although his corporate image is neat and tidy, personally he is a free spirit who is a bit of a 'clutter-bug' and a 'loner.' A 'Potential Patty' sees his corporate career path as the best choice, and thinks that she can remove some of the clutter, and tame the free spirit within him to fit HER vision of the future. And although he may be game for her ideas and suggestions, upon realizing that she is attempting to change him-the relationship is destined for a failure or a difficult time ahead.

Just remember that in the meeting phase of dating, assume NOTHING. Do not assume that he is heterosexual. Do not assume that because he is approaching you that he is single. Do not assume that because he does not speak of children, that he does not have any. Do not assume anything. Ask, but do not make it feel like an interview or an interrogation. Be direct and deliberate to get the answers you NEED to let you know what you are dealing with. This also ties into the prior Chapter of Knowing Thy Self, considering that once you open this door to receive the information from him – you, in turn, must be able to share the same of yourself. If he lies, that is on him as a person, but if you do not ask, that is on you as woman for not seeking the truth.

THE DATING SCENE IS CRAZY

Chapter 3

(Rant)

I watch my single friends and family go through their pitfalls of attempting to find someone that they have something remotely in common with. Then there are the others that come out of a relationship trying to re-single-ize themselves, only to realize that what they had was far better than being out on the prowl with the vultures. From jobs to clubs to church to working out, a single person is always on the hunt (consciously or subconsciously) for a prospect at prosperity, peace of mind, and that elusive 'happily ever after.' Searching, hunting, waiting, praying, chanting for a mate. Because in the end, no matter how 'hard' we want to be - we all want to be loved for who we are.

It seems the longer people are single, the more set in their ways they are. Holding themselves hostage, releasing parts of who they are and even less of what they are about. I tend to use the term 'jaded'. They want it, but whomever they meet has to go through hell to see a glimpse of something promising. Some sick single person's version of 'hazing.' "I can be the best man/woman for you, but...umm...you gotta go first." You have to show how much you want it, but you don't even know what the 'it' is that you are getting. I am not sure who began the 'hedging your bets' process on dating, but it is out of control.

Men: Have gotten so comfortable with the fact that there is 'available man shortage' that they do and say almost anything. Enjoying the fruits of meaningless sex with single and non-single women alike, and nurturing an ever-growing fear of commitment. If he is a top notch catch, he knows it, and every woman will know it as well by his follow up question to the woman, "Well, what do you bring to the table?" Her resume' best be long and distinguished to compete with his fear of potential damage to his good credit rating, moving her into his home-or selling his, and changing the direction of what has gotten him this far - all for the sake of a chance at love. Then there is the man who isn't hitting on two pennies, but for some reason the ladies love him. So why should he commit? He is getting all of the benefits from multiple women and none of the responsibilities. Jaded from one end of the spectrum to the other.

Women: Have become so empowered via economic needs, products of broken homes, or equal opportunity; that many have become somewhat unapproachable. Electing "group think" and "yeah girl" groups as opposed to the potential of a meaningful relationship for fear of being emotionally injured. Good male prospects are slim, so the protection mechanism is operating on a high level. If she is top notch typically she is 'self-contained' and demanding to avoid a poser. Overlooking the garbage man, simply because he IS the garbage man. A road to being superficial yet seeking substance - won't work. And then there is the woman who determines that her 'sex' is her way of self-fulfillment. Sexing the single man, the married man, or any man in hopes to lure him her way. Committing sexually in hopes that it develops into an emotional commitment. But if it doesn't work - no loss on her part, as she benefits in a way similar to her male counterpart. But why would he commit to her? (see above paragraph) Jaded on this side of the fence too.

Where do we begin in an effort to pull it together? It seems as if there are more singles being added daily to this war of attrition. And there is no winner. Both sides are getting further apart. Digging in deeper and drawing battle lines to protect their hearts. For those that are in a relationship or married....STAY THERE....there is nothing to see here, keeping it moving. Grab your mate's hand and walk away briskly to avoid the 'jaded' bug.

MEN TO AVOID

Chapter 4

Women often warn other women off from different types of men, but rarely have a legitimate reason as to why. As a man sharing information, let me share a few types of men or male situations to avoid.

<u>The Angry Man/Trouble Man</u>

He is always angry or has an issue in your presence. He really does not have an issue (exaggerated/lies), but his demeanor appeals to a woman's nurturing nature. His demeanor also allows him to control how close you can or cannot become to him. By appealing to your nurturing side, it becomes easy for you to take on his causes, sometimes more than he does. In the midst of HIS confusion many women develop a feeling of obligation to his problems, and will tend to overlook the issues of THAT man. He may be flawed in many ways, but purposefully masks those major flaws with dramatic propaganda to keep you off balance.

It is a patented 'male pity party' that endears the woman to him and keeps her connected through the ruse (deception) of feeling needed. Don't try to save him. Your efforts to save him is the bait and you are the fish.

Sniff him out early ladies. A true man down on his luck will not look to you to correct his issues. He will be in the process of correcting them and producing tangible results for him…not you.

The Vague Visionary

He is the man you meet who is very suave and debonair. He offers a hint of mystery in everything he does, but is never direct about anything. The Vague Visionary will offer 'fortune cookie' answers with minimal substance; however he will typically have you thinking about what it is he just said. His available time will seem minimal, but this coupled with his vague answers is also a way of drawing you in, without any sense of mutual commitment on his part. He is the guy you will date for six months and realize that you know absolutely nothing about him.

To recognize him you have to discern between privacy/discretion and dodging a question. This goes back to asking direct Core Questions that can yield tangible answers. The Vague Visionary will either become defensive or just not interact with you to avoid revealing that his actual person does not match his initially presented representative.

The Needy Ned

Needy Ned is the Angry/Trouble man, minus the sad or angry faces. Ned typically is full speed ahead. He tells you how much he needs you to accomplish his goals. His calm yet pleading approach creates the same draw or play on the desire to feel needed. So, don't try to save Ned either.

Needy Neds typically are dreamers without a plan. If he does have a plan, typically that plan involves a heavy dose of you to make it happen. Needy Ned's tend to be 'moochers' as well. They borrow resources with no intent of repaying.

Although it is great to feel needed, a man with a plan for success will strive for it regardless of who is in or out of his life. He may have a few setbacks, but his goals are not contingent upon the woman he is with.

<u>Project Paul</u>

He is a jack of all trades but master of none. Project Pauls typically have commitment issues, and this is evident by their numerous projects. These type of men seem very intriguing and full of potential, but you have to ask yourself two questions:

(1) Where do I fit in to all of that; and

(2) Will I be replaced by the next best project?

If you think you have met a Project Paul, you will only learn that he is one by the disappointments related to broken promises and poor time management. Try to determine early if he has too many irons in the fire, and possibly unable to be the man you need/desire.

As you are already aware, men come in all shapes and sizes, so this is only a few men to try and avoid. Again, be diligent and direct in your getting to know phase.

PUTTING YOU UP ON GAME

Chapter 5

Avoid The Gray – clarity is key.

In many cases it is to a man's advantage to allow things to 'just flow' or 'see where it takes us.' I call it "The Gray". It allows some men a pre-screening of a woman to see if things can develop into a relationship. The Gray can also allow other men, who have no plans of commitment, to benefit from a woman who desires more, and is presenting her best efforts to fulfill those desires. It is important to avoid the latter.

Refer back to the section on Core Questions, and ensure your fact finding process is sound. Keep in mind that in the initial meeting, things will be new, and full of unknowns. That process should not last long. The time frame will depend on how much time is available to get to know each other. Busy schedules and physical distance may hinder the ability to spend time, thus the time frame may be longer. Congruent schedules and aggressive time spending acts can shorten this time frame dramatically.

This is the point where most women error. There is a desire to know where things are headed, but an even greater desire to not rock the boat of good vibes and run him off. It is imperative that the desire to not rock the boat does not overshadow the need for clarity. The Gray is like a fog.

Once she is aware that the man of her interest is who she wants to date or be with exclusively, she should arrange a moment of clarity. This moment should be a comfortable setting. Preferably an activity that allows for some one-on-one alone time to talk. At the opportune time she should, in an unemotional way, express the fact that she has a genuine interest in him, enjoys his company, insert a few compliments, and that she desires to be 'exclusive' with him. She should give him a few days to consider her offer, and set a date and time to meet and discuss his thoughts. If he desires to answer then, she should let him. If he follows her lead to wait, then she should pick the current dating encounter back up with the same vibe and energy prior to the conversation.

A few points to be noted here, her unemotional expression is a way to avoid creating an overwhelming feeling for the man. If she is in control, then it keeps the potential tension down, and keeps him focused on the words being said. Also, she is expressing her thoughts and reasons in efforts to create dialogue to ensure that, going forward, there is no room for misunderstandings. The follow up date is set to also alleviate the pressure to answer on the spot. In most cases, the woman can complete all of this without the man uttering a single word– keeping her in control until it is time for him to respond.

A moment of clarity should be provided early on to avoid investing too much into a situation that may not develop. One can become emotionally attached to someone and fall victim to The Gray for the sake of continuing the good feeling they have become accustomed to. This moment of clarity can also be altered to address other issues within relationships.

It is with this clarity that a woman can proceed as SHE sees fit.

Avoid nicknames/Pet names

In getting to know a man, during blissful periods of its 'newness' it is common to create nicknames and pet names for each other. Try to avoid these, or at least avoid the overuse of them until a commitment is established.

Terms such as those can allow a woman to feel closer to a man, as they lend to thoughts of endearment, closeness, and a feeling of being special. Allow him to use other ways to express this. A man who is a "player" will use these terms in an interchangeable fashion with various women, thus these terms of endearment have very little meaning to him. Yet, they mean much more to the women.

If there are signs of use before a commitment is agreed upon sway him (initially) back to using your name. Use statements such as: "I like the way you say MY name better" or "MY name sounds better than any nickname you could come up with…..for now." In the event he is persistent with you using a nickname/pet name then in a formal and direct way express your desire that he use YOUR name instead. In the end, such a request should not be asking too much.

Promote Transparency

Some people are 'nosey' or natural snoopers, but typically if they are with someone who is transparent, that characteristic will rarely show itself. Transparent is defined as: transmitting light so that objects or images can be seen as if there were no intervening material; easily seen through or detected; or obvious.

We are all skeptical of the information we provide when meeting new people. Stalkers and mentally unstable individuals within our society is a reality. It is suggested that you offer the outline of transparency to the man that you become interested in. If you have issues with trusting people, express: *that in a committed relationship, if you pick up his phone when it rings– it should not be a problem; if you pick up his phone to play a phone game –it's not an issue; or if information is requested – it should not be a problem….even if never used.*

By promoting the transparency you desire in a committed relationship, a man can choose if that is something he can compromise on or not. And as you continue to get to know each other, he is prepared for the requirements, effort, and understanding that it will take to make the relationship work.

Lead by example. Be what you desire character-wise

For the 'Promoting Transparency' section to be successful, you must lead by example. It is unfair and a certain recipe for disaster to ask of a man (or anyone for that matter) to do what you are NOT willing to do yourself.

If you want to be spoiled, spoil him. If you want to feel appreciated, appreciate him. If you want communication, then communicate with him. If you want respect, respect him.

There will be some criticism of the prior paragraph. The response to those criticisms will be the following:

If you are being true to yourself, then the examples above of how you treat your man, are a reflection of you. If you are unwilling to give freely of yourself due to what he may or may not be providing; then it will always create a serious level of difficulty to achieve the relationship you so desire. Be who YOU are. Be the woman (future wife) that YOU desire to be. Keep in mind that those things require

YOU to be honest with YOU about what YOU want, and how YOU plan to get there. He is (or should be) your equal, so promote the interaction as such.

If there is a conversation later about him not reciprocating, you will have references to your words, which will be supported by your previous actions. Since those actions will be a direct result of who you are and what you desire, they will be genuine to the core.

Don't allow a negative precedence to be set

Often times when couples come together, there is a change within an existing relationship based on growing expectations. Avoid change that sets a negative precedence. Once set, the precedence becomes a relationship norm, and eats away at the relationship from the inside.

Prior to addressing any issue, one must TRULY weigh out if this 'issue' is something worthy of making a stance on. Not folding the bath towels in a fashion that you desire is not a negative precedence, it is a preference. So choose wisely.

If he stays out all night until the following morning, and that is a problem for you, it is best to address that the first time it happens as opposed to overlooking it.

Now there is a way to address it. And that way should be in a non-threatening tone that promotes understanding instead of an argument. It is important to be firm in your stance but not accusatory in your dialogue. Explain why it is upsetting to you and that you 'do not desire to be in a relationship where someone purposefully upsets you.' That quote is a way to put the focus on the result of the action as opposed to the action itself. If the action is continued on without an effort for a compromise, then you have a decision to make. Again, ensure that your issue is reasonable before placing you both in an uncomfortable situation. Think first, then speak to avoid words you cannot take back.

Don't let the low number of men allow you to become a statistic

You will often hear many women reference the low number of 'available' men. The term 'available' is relative, but the subject itself is very real. There are a number of women out there that consistently find themselves in bad relationships due to being lonely. The fact that they ARE 'lonely' turns them into 'over-lookers', thus settling with someone to battle away the feeling of being alone.

This goes back to Knowing Thy Self, and sticking to who YOU are. Will you meet friends and associates of the opposite sex along the way? Of course! However, it is probably not in your best interest to rationalize your way into dating them if they do not possess what you need and desire. It is unfair to them and ultimately selfish to do so.

Imagine falling for a guy only to learn months later that he is really not that into you. That you were only taking up space and time because he was tired of being alone. Would have respected him more for saving you the heartache? Probably.

Good/great sex does not equal a good/great person for you.

Don't get "dickmatized"

We have all heard the conversation of abstaining from sex until marriage, and I am sure we all can agree that the decisions of when and how to have sex rest solely on the shoulders of each individual. The following is for those that choose pre-marital sex of some kind.

In my numerous conversations it is an all too re-occurring theme with many women, that good or pleasurable sex is not a consistently common occurrence. Hence good sex encounters can have effects similar to that of a person with an addiction. Chasing that 'high'.

Rationalizing her way into reducing her standards, ignoring her Hierarchy of Ten, and discarding her Deal Breaker Ten at the opportunity to continue to feel the great physical pleasure. Dickmatized. Throwing caution to the wind to satisfy that sexual itch that it seems only he can scratch. Dickmatized. Finding yourself not caring if the interaction is slowing you down from your goals/plans or is ultimately unhealthy. It feels good right now and better than what you have experienced. Dickmatized; Sprung; Nose Open; or whatever term you desire – it rarely works out well if she-you loses yourself in the process.

It is true that the value of sexual compatibility is grossly understated by most women, but extremely important. However, great sex does NOT mean he is or will be a good mate for you. Some women will initially decide to have sex with a man continuously in hopes that those encounters will result in a relationship. If no one else has told you, I will tell you: most men can have sex without emotion; some men can have sex with a woman for an extended time frame, and never develop deeper feelings for her; and some men will say many things to enhance their chances of sleeping with you.

In short, ladies, if you choose to have pre-marital or casual sex, make an effort to do so on your own terms. Keep your wits about you, and have your Hierarchy of Ten/Deal Breaker Ten lists accessible. If he covers your lists and desires with more than just the sex, then you have something to build on and work with. Otherwise, tread lightly and BE SAFE.

HIS-STORY

Chapter 6

In recognizing the fundamental differences between men and women, the thing that is consistently overlooked are the distinct differences that drives them. The ability to continue to recognize that difference is a key component in knowing him, communicating with him, sex, love, and longevity.

As with anyone, a man's past/upbringing is a key component to the current product he is, and the finished product he will become. It is common for women to overlook this aspect of the men they decide to get to know. If a woman chooses to accept him for who he is, it is imperative for her to listen, learn, process, and understand how he came to be. In addition to learning his process of how he will choose to move forward. Of course you will not want to know the history of every man you casually meet, but as a relationship begins to bud into desires to become mutually exclusive keep HIS history in mind.

You should want to know if he was he raised by a single or dual parent household? If single, was the absent parent active in his life? A man raised with minimal parental influence can encounter development struggles along the way. He may consistently run into having to learn many things on his own. If such a trend of self-learning is necessary, it can create communication barriers even for those closest to him. A certain level of pride grows with successful self-learning, and such pride is not easily put aside at the first opportunity of a relationship. It has gotten him to the point of attracting you, so in his mind he has done just fine.

In this example, it is better to understand and enhance the 'why', as opposed to abrupt efforts to change his process.

Also, the household is where most men see their examples of male-female relationships, how to treat women, and a sense of family.

The examples of male-female relationships will either cause him to mimic what he has seen, or go in the opposite direction of it. Depending on his example, this can be either good or bad. This should offer insight into his views on how relationships should proceed. It won't cover everything, but a peek into his core values is always beneficial.

Early lessons of manners and examples of chivalry may shape how he determines a woman should be treated. If his mother consistently was abused it can either push him towards being a protector or an abuser himself. If the single mother parades her various male interests around in front of him, he could choose to be a protector, but more than likely will have very little respect for the women he encounters.

Despite the family structure during his upbringing, how he views the aspect of family will affect most of his future relationships. If family is important to him it could affect his availability. From the momma's boy to the loner, the connection or tie to them is and will be evident.

Many relationships start off with 'surface' questions. And later a woman will ask herself...how well does she really know this man? As he shares more and more of himself, whether initially or later on in the relationship, there are key things to consider.

• What type of relationship does he have with his father and mother? This is important, as it will offer insight into his development. Absence of father and moderate relationship with mother will typically lean toward him having to learn many lessons on his own. This can create a strong sense of self, aggressive attitude, or unyielding drive. He is comfortable with his methods, as they have served him well. It will take a strong woman to handle him; as he will challenge many things that cross his path. Absence of father and a strong bond with mother tends to offer more openness to ideas and change, yet less assertive. Absence of father in both scenarios lends to underlying pain that cannot be ignored. A strong bond with father is the wild card. Depending upon the father's personality there can either be a strong well rounded man, or a shell of a strong well rounded man. Some father's allow their sons develop naturally, and others will place expectations upon them that they spend their entire lives trying to live up to. Through continued dialogue about the father, you will be able to determine which. Finally, a healthy dose of both parents drives balance.

• What type of father will he be or is he? We have all heard the stories of the estranged 'baby mother' who keeps the child away from the man. Be sure this is the case in the event his children are not part of his life. If they are not in his life by HIS choosing, ask why. Extending unconditional love to his child means that he is capable of extending and receiving unconditional love from others.

• What are his goals? Not just the talked about goals. Not just the 'wish I was rich' goal. The goals that have merit, a plan to accomplish them, and the drive to attempt them. Whether it is aspirations to be President, or goals of becoming the lifelong employee in a desired profession; you can make the determination if those goals can be aligned with yours. It also will assist in your ability to be able to support those goals.

• Find out or recognize his emotional baggage. This term is commonly used concerning women, but men have emotional baggage as well. He will guard it with his life, so finding it out will be no easy task. Every man finds a way to deal with their emotional pain, but most do not deal with it directly to find a resolution. It is no secret that men tend to NOT be the best communicators. Expressions of failure, denial, trust, concern, are all neatly compartmentalized away thus making it tougher on women to be supportive and both parties reaching the root of the problem. Despite this lack of ability to communicate effectively, it is essential to any relationship of merit. Communication is also listening effectively. A woman must ensure she is doing her part to hear her man. Look for ways to be creative.

• Always present yourself as open to him. Available for conversation. Compare it to the availability you would present to your child – open and without judgment. A comfort level makes him feel that his secrets are safe with you.

• When in engaged in a conversation, gauge his mood. If he is excited, let him talk and share as much as he can - uninterrupted. Men hate to be interrupted. Only when he is finished, ask questions that fill in the blanks. If he is withdrawn or not as forthcoming, ask open ended questions that lead into a conversation. Be careful not to give him a reason to retreat. This aspect goes back to the section on Leading By Example. Hopefully once recognized, he will be that same safe space for you.

Long story short…take your time and learn. No assumptions.

THE MALE PHYSICAL MENTALITY

Chapter 7

In order to fully understand this area, it must be prefaced a little bit. Open your mind to be able to remove many of the things about men that you were told. Keeping that open mind is going to be key to the following information. Women are approached in a sexual manner early in their lives and often. The ability to find a sexual partner is quite easy. It is the double standard social view of a woman with numerous partners, and the ability to find a satisfying partner that drives many women over the edge.

Hence, there is no pressure from early adulthood well into later life concerning sex. This can be a good and/or a bad thing.

For those women who learn to embrace their sexuality it can be positive, as it allows them to appreciate their sexual nature. To wear it, flaunt it, experiment with it, and enjoy the confidence that embracing their sexual nature brings.

On the other end of the spectrum, denouncing her sexuality can create considerable reservations, use of sex as a tool for other gains, or complete detachment from one of the more beautiful aspects of womanhood.

Men on the other hand, are not so fortunate. They are not the pursued, hence always chasing a woman. So there is considerable pressure not only to be successful in pursuit, but also to be successful in performance. This pressure has caused most men to become selfish lovers, who are more thrilled with the conquest; and consistently shortchanging their female partners from their potential pleasure. It is this pressure that causes men to rank sex higher on their 'Hierarchy of Ten' than women.

For the women who have not embraced their sensual/sexual side, this distinct difference in ranking or lack of recognition, creates a consistent discord within the relationship. Sex may make a woman's top ten, but the average man ranks sex in their top three.

In many cases of the men that cheat, this is a key driver, as something within the relationship has slowed or stopped sexual activity altogether. For women that use sex as a form of control– they lose, as the next opportunity for sexual expression and gratification for the man will become even more tempting than before.

In understanding this aspect of men, a compromise must be met. If sex is number two on his list, and number six on her list…find a happy medium at four. This compromise is an ongoing process as it will require both parties to be patient, attentive, selfless, and above all else honest.

A comedian once joked that good sex may get a car note or the rent paid, but excellent oral will get you a home. This is stated only as an example of how crucial the ranking of sex is to men.

A close friend of mine began to worry about her man's actions on the nights he went out with the guys (most of whom were single), as they would stay out late into the night. She began to wonder if he might be tempted to stray. I suggested to her the idea of sex or oral sex prior to him going out, ensuring that he climaxes. Thus removing the potential sexual pressure or pinned up energy or stress. I also advised her to avoid arguments prior to his departure. Arguments cause the body to release adrenaline and cortisol. So upon ending the argument, the body must be calmed down or the tension released. In efforts to calm down the man may talk more, drink more, and/or be more aggressive in nature to relieve the tension. These ingredients are prime additives for making a man susceptible to the advances from other women, or advancing on his own. So avoid the 'pre-guys night out argument' all together. She was hesitant at first, but now he goes out less, or when he does – he is eager to get home for round two.

Each man is different, and that goes without saying, but one cannot stress enough the importance level of each woman's understanding about her man's sexual desires/needs, and how to customize her approach to meeting those desires/needs.

For women in relationships/marriages with children, the time and effort must continuously be made to engage in sexual activity and display sex appeal. It should be just as important as eating, showering, working, paying bills, etc. The common commentary of men is the decline in a woman's sex drive and show of sexiness as time progresses. As a woman you may change over time (weight gain or loss being most common), but presentation of self must still be there. It is pertinent to carry yourself in a way that appeals to your man, as well as what makes you feel good about you. If he is a leg man, accentuate your legs. If he is a breast man, accentuate those. But never, I repeat….NEVER become too busy to be sexy for yourself AND your man. This advice is more beneficial to you as a woman to keep you feeling good about you, and the by-product is a man who cannot keep his eyes or hands off of you. Although he may appreciate your ability to relax and dress down, be conscious of how you choose to dress down. From sleep wear, to work out gear, to cleaning apparel, to the clothes you wear to work – be sexy for yourself as well as him.

If you are watching the football game together (just the two of you) wear the Jersey only, or comfortable pants and a top that shows you off. As for sleep wear choose the more sensual apparel as opposed to the flannel pajamas. Men are visual creatures, and such actions do not go unnoticed. I do advise being prepared for the response that may come with such actions. No need to dangle the prize but not be prepared to pay up.

Of course this may not be available in all scenarios, but men tend to have short attention spans– so although you may or may not physically be where you want to be you cannot isolate yourself physically and sexually from him.

As the saying goes, what one will not do, another one will. I suggest that ALL women have an internally competitive motor. A desire to please your man past where he desires to be pleased, and then make efforts to surpass that level. They say a 'happy wife makes for a happy life', and there is not a grammatically correct saying for a man or husband to fit that theme, but striving to make him just as happy as you desire to be, should be priority.

Most men know what they desire sexually, but are hesitant about being an initiator of sharing. He does not want to seem raw or raunchy, so he may withhold ideas. Women often ask why men sneak and watch pornography...this is in part why.

They will rarely crack the door of opportunity to discuss, so attempt to secure a level of comfort to avoid a conversational retreat on his part -thus resulting in a total loss of the effort to share. You can also initiate with sharing of what you desire sexually, and then in turn ask of him. Many men respect a woman for her level of comfort with her sexuality. This can make it easier for him to keep open the lines of communication concerning your sex life.

Just as you would want him to make the top items on your 'Hierarchy of Ten' his priority, so should you. This also goes back to leading by example. The impact is immeasurable.

EGO

Chapter 8

Contrary to popular belief the male ego is as fragile as an uncooked egg. This uncooked egg is surrounded by a cushion of bravado, social expectations, and a continuing dose of self-preservation. This (EGO) contributes to men being emotionally detached; in efforts to live up to what is the common belief of what a man should be. Men do not cry. Men do not show signs of weakness. Men are to be dominant. Men are the breadwinner. Men are always in control. Anything less, and (inside looking out) from a society's vantage point he is less than a man. And in the end – being a man is all that a man has, or so is believed. So strap on your stiletto hiking boots ladies because it is an uphill battle, cradling this ego with the care of a small child, but the respect of an equal. Reminder: Keep an open mind.

No matter how great a man is or can be, he can only be as great as the woman beside him. And to be that woman, you must understand and accept that your role is ever-changing.

You must be the 'Magic' Johnson of woman-hood (basketball analogy) for the man that you choose to move forward with. Magic Johnson played all five positions for the Los Angeles Lakers, because that is what his team needed at the time. And he delivered. In the 1980 finals, Game 6, Kareem Abdul-Jabbar could not play due to a sprained ankle. The coach started Magic at center. Through the course of the game he also played guard and forward, finishing with 42 points, 15 rebounds, 7 assists, and three steals as the Lakers won 123 to 107. He recognized the situations, played to his strengths, and improved his weaknesses to become the All-star his team needed. With your man, to combat his ego's shell, you must become HIS All-star. How much of an effort this will require will vary from man to man.

Some days he may need a caregiver, some days he needs a woman to be in control and trust that she can handle her/their business. Then some days, he will need her to be submissive so he can take the lead.

Sounds like work? It is. What is the alternative? Lack of communication, gaps in connection, fights, or worse……a damaged egg.

Pause. Now some women are asking: Why should I do all of this? Why should I put forth such effort? What is he going to be doing?

The response: Why not? There will be men that are not worthy of such efforts. There will be men who are worthy but may fail to appreciate such efforts. However, when you encounter each opportunity for a successful relationship, hopefully this insight helps you maintain who YOU are by doing what comes naturally. Withholding your efforts due to fear is the same as the chance that is never taken - you will never know how it would have ended or better yet....never ended. Let us continue.

A crushed or battered ego can cause a man to withdraw and/or seek 'ego-building' activities elsewhere. (Cheating) In withdrawing it can affect communication, affection, intimacy, and total mood. His defenses are up and every situation has the potential to escalate. His resentment for what has damaged his ego will be a huge hurdle to overcome, and almost insurmountable should that source of his pain be you. This is why it tends to be harder for men to forgive women who cheat on them.

Men are rare participants in depression, so in the best interest of self-preservation, the ego has to be rebuilt as soon as possible. Immediate gratification is a must. A comfort level must be reached. A genuine compliment from another woman or family goes a very long way at this point. He will be resistant to your attempts to repair the damage if you are the source, but you will have to be persistent and consistent in being available. Allowing him to have space during this time is a slippery slope. You cannot smother him, but you also cannot give him too much freedom as he will assume you do not care. A man with a damaged ego rarely will give clues or directions on how to help him heal. Hopefully you can avoid this scenario altogether.

Many of you have heard the term, 'let a man be a man'. This term originally was created to allow men to keep their egos intact. It has evolved over time to encompass many other aspects of assumed male behavior, but the initial premise is based in a good place.

The rise in the independence of women has affected this saying in many ways. Self-sufficient stances via broken homes (single mothers) and great strides in the work place have empowered women to new heights. Those successes have not translated into advancement in the relationship arena. Some women have allowed it to alter their male-female relationships by becoming so independent that their success are lorded over the men they meet. The male ego, for most men, is behind the curve in adjusting. In a situation where both parties are very successful, both have to remember that they are more than just their individual successes. At the end of the day, they have to remember that men and women are still just human.

Although the male stigma is to be strong and impregnable, men enjoy compliments and encouragement as well. In fact it is needed. Just as a woman desires positive tones and support, so do men. Many women call this 'stroking his ego', but you must be careful in this arena. It has to come from a genuine place.

Empty compliments will eventually be revealed, and the feeling of being 'mocked' sets in. Withdrawal.

The key to the male Ego is trust. The same trust that allows one's heart to be vulnerable is the trust required for a man to let his guard down. This trust is not easily earned. A man can love a woman with all that he has, but still be guarded with his core. A great woman can be trustworthy, but certain acts or traits can result in reservations about him being exposed in this area.

A key example would be gossip. "If she will talk about other folks, will she talk about us? Can I trust that?" A man will never tell you that he wonders this. He will just be cautious about what he does and what he shares. He wants to trust you to keep his secrets….secret. Nothing is worse than having your weakness put on display by the person you love in the heat of a disagreement. Words, once spoken, are free. I strongly suggest never using his secrets against him. The trust will be lost forever.

That is enough about the Male Ego. It may sound challenging. Some are more challenging than others, but the point remains that making an effort to understand the Male Ego is essential in understanding the man you are with. Let's move forward.

OLD FASHIONED ADVANTAGE

Chapter 9

The continuous change culture-wise has caused many relationship functions to no longer be carried out by traditional genders. Women are no longer 'just' homemakers and housewives. Men are no longer the only or primary source of family income. The necessity born out of survival and broken homes are consistently challenging the traditional relationship roles.

With more single men learning survival techniques from single mothers, there is not a 'need' or even a 'requirement' for a woman to aid in the cooking and home making aspects. Men do not harp on women's cooking ability as they once did in the past. Men simply cook and fend for themselves. However, now that many men have become successful with their cooking skills, a woman who can cook does not have the advantage that she once did. A woman lacking in this area is viewed at an even greater disadvantage. He may not need a woman to cook a four-course meal daily, but knowing that she can and will is a seldom mentioned desire for many men.

The desire of a well-rounded woman (remember Magic Johnson reference) is rooted in the traditional values of relationships. He does not want a servant, but he does desire to be catered to and/or taken care of by his woman. If her heart is truly into the relationship then this aspect will come easy. If the skill is not there, the will to do so can drive the woman to seek out ways to enhance her abilities.

Independent. One can no longer tell if being an independent woman is a good or bad thing. If a woman does not have some level of independence then she may be less desirable due to her personal need to depend on her mate. If a woman is overly independent she can come off as not desiring a man because she may not need one. Hence unapproachable. Ultimately this area is conquered by three things: (1) balance, (2) purpose, and (3) presentable versatility.

Balance is essential in the area of independence IF a woman desires companionship. Just as a woman desires balance of her man, the same is desired of a potential woman. Being needy is not attractive to most men. It does feed their ego early on, but this victory is short lived. Very few men desire to be 'controlled' like a house pet who is taken out for convenience purposes, then stored away. Men, just like many women, desire to feel needed, but yet supported. Hence, balance. Think on that.

Purpose is defined as the reason for which something exists, is done, is made, etc. Simply put, purpose is THE reason why. If one recognizes and more importantly, remembers their purpose in a relationship, the pitfalls of independence, selfishness, ego, and pride all fall away for the greater good of the relationship. Purpose within the relationship helps define our roles to us and to our mates. It is that purpose which creates and maintains the common goal of the couple. As you date and move in and out of relationships, your role may vary.

Presentable Versatility is the ability to move effectively in any environment. My grandmother often spoke of how a woman should conduct herself in public, regardless of the situation. Men who know better, seek better. How a woman handles herself will always make a difference in how she is approached, treated, and revered. As I have stated, men are visual creatures, but leave a bit to the imagination. There is a time and a place for everything. A good woman can determine those times. A great woman can determine, act, and flourish during those times. Discretion is key. This outward approach of discretion compliments the male ego on many levels. Give that some thought as well.

Make sure you are fully comfortable with a mature set of standards and morals. There will be many who attempt to change them, alter them, and lower them. When you have a true understanding of the 'why' (purpose) behind your standards, then you will always be able to lean on them during times of uncertainty. The 'high road' is the one seldom traveled, but it will make the difference in the quality of men that will be attracted to you.

If one wants the marriage/relationship longevity that was abundant with our grand and great-grand parents, it is best to lean on some of those traditional relationship values.

WHY MEN CHEAT

Chapter 10

Let's first address the obvious. Some men cheat because they are greedy and do not care about the woman's feelings. They are mean and hurtful people. Some do it intentionally (do not care), others unintentionally (hope to never get caught). There are men, who can be classified as 'sex' addicts and no matter how much a woman has sex with them – it will never be enough. We see these individuals daily and although they do not make up the majority, those seemingly have shaped the perception of men in general. So now that we have moved the percentage of men who cheat for those reasons to the side, we can dive into why the average man may possibly cheat on his woman as opposed to removing himself from the relationship altogether.

Let's start at the beginning. Men are well behind the physical and sexual curve in comparison to women. It starts with childhood. Women reach puberty sooner, so they become more aware of their bodies at a younger age. Young girls (even as they become young women) are attracted to older males due to levels of maturity. Their male counterparts have yet to reach an equal level of mental stability concerning male-female interaction.

Reiterating, men arrive at puberty later and shortly thereafter (early twenties) they begin peaking sexually. Women reach puberty earlier than men, but do not begin to peak until they reach their early-to-mid thirties. Some women suggest an even higher sexual crest in their early forties. Women have more time to be able to accept and process the changes physically and mentally before beginning to peak. Managing it effectively as the 'pursued' and in some cases, going months or years without sexual activity. The window from puberty to peak for men is so small that the majority never reach such a level of self-understanding. So they follow the instinctive approach sexually, learning as they go, but driven by a 'conquest' sexual appetite.

Women are advanced upon sexually early and often in life. So much so that women become immune to the subtle sexual advances. The smiles, stares, compliments, helpfulness, and general niceness are all extensions of men testing the waters. Some women enjoy the attention and relish in it. Others swat them away so often it almost becomes second nature.

Most men are not advanced upon early in life, and it seldom happens in early adulthood. Men are the hunter as opposed to the hunted, but women are typically in the sexual driver's seat of the car named 'desire'. And it will only go as far as she wants it to.

Whether a man's sex drive is high or low, sex is another pre-conceived notion of manhood. It is instilled early on that the 'guy' who has sex with the most girls is popular, socially accepted, envied, and desired. Many women have stepped outside of their normal routines to have sex with a man because his sexual reputation precedes him. Whether it is the 'Notches on the belt' analogy, or the "Sexual race to the top" scenario, until a maturity level is reached, these myths concerning the 'stairway to manhood' will continue to drive men's sexual appetite.

It is relatively easy for men to secure instant gratification. Men, unlike women typically reach full sexual climax with each sexual encounter. Couple such a release with previously mentioned pre-conceived notions, and a man instantly feels better physically and mentally about himself. Excessive stress normally lowers the libido, and sex is the virtual 'fix-it' pill, in the minds of most men. I advise women to never send their men away carrying stress of any kind, as he may look to relieve this stress with a sexual encounter.

Reminder, men are visual creatures. Physical properties rarely go unnoticed. From smiles, to eyes, to breast, to hips, to hands, to attire, and/or feet, men recognize and appreciate. Even if it is not verbally expressed or expressed correctly, it is taken into the mental memory banks.

Many women are reading this and saying to themselves, "He does not recognize or appreciate MY physical." He does appreciate and recognize it, but one has to ask that woman, "Do you keep your man's eyes on you with the way you dress, walk, talk, and carry yourself?" "Do you present yourself in a positive fashion as often as humanly possible?" In the everyday life of career, kids, health, keeping up a house, etc. the answer is probably 'NO'. In most cases a comfort level has settled in and a belief that he has seen you at your best, so he KNOWS what he is getting. That may be true, but it is imperative that you SHOW him what HE has on a consistent basis. He should never have to refer to his memory on how physically appealing you are to him.

Years ago I was speaking with a woman who had been a lifetime house wife. Her husband would leave very early in the morning for work. She would cook, clean, and care for the children during the day, but she stated that she always made it a point to be dressed and looking her best when he arrived home from work. She cared and catered for him daily, but stated that her doing this was a key component to her marriage, as it always gave him something to visually look forward to when headed home.

Men are very aware that there is a 'decent man shortage.' It is almost to the point where it is just a man shortage period. A man doesn't have to carry the credentials of the past to be considered a good man. With the openness of gay men, increase in inter-racial dating, increase of men in prison, heightened fear of men on the 'down-low', and men that just don't care to progress – the male selection pools have shrunk dramatically. And men know it.

Such a man shortage has caused women to feel comfortable with sharing a man. The old adage that something is better than nothing tends to show up here. The men that are cheating are cheating with someone, and typically that someone knows that she is the other woman.

People cheat, but the Internet and social media has widened the accessibility to people who may not be as restrained as others. In most cases, it starts off with catching up with old friends. Somewhere between catching up and meeting new people, the lack of self-restraint is exposed. If you refer back to the beginning of this chapter you will notice it was stated that men are behind the sexual curve, and that men are typically the hunter. Such access creates a target-rich environment.

Gravy On My Steak

A term I coined many years ago, only to realize later that many men (and women) cheat this way. A properly cooked steak requires nothing extra. It is the main course. No steak sauce of any kind is needed. And once you have had a properly cooked steak, nothing else will suffice. But if you are truly craving a steak, and it is not prepared to your expectations, you will work with it to satisfy your desire…..adding whatever condiment that makes it acceptable to you. In this analogy the steak is your significant other, and the condiment (Gravy) is the person or persons outside of your relationship.

He has no desire on leaving the woman he is with, but he does desire to enhance what she may be lacking, has lost, or is unwilling to do. This commonly happens during a lengthy disconnect where he is unable to express the shortcoming, or has expressed what it is and the effort to meet the need is not there. The desire does not manifest itself into a conscious decision to seek alternate company, but an openness to entertain advances that he might have otherwise ignored. In many cases, the 'gravy' fulfills the desire to feel needed or wanted. She wants his time and attention, whereas the significant other may have become complacent.

You are probably asking yourself: why doesn't the cheater just leave? The Gravy is not and can never be the main course. So mentally the cheater is attempting to enhance their own well-being by filling in the minor gaps in the main relationship. The common rational is that the main relationship will improve and The Gravy will no longer be needed. Remember, we are talking about the average person, not the habitual cheater.

Remember earlier where we discussed keeping his eyes and focus on you? And didn't we touch upon self-gratification for men? Pull those items into this thought process. Add a lack of or breakdown in communication. Hopefully the picture is coming together.

In the end, he should be strong enough to stay faithful, as well as she should not desire to leave anything to chance by becoming complacent. However, we all are human. And in a perfect world both are remaining focused for the sake of the relationship.

All cheating is wrong. From emotional cheating to physical cheating, no one deserves it. But it does happen. These people are cheating with someone, and in many cases the other parties are aware. It takes two.

SUMMARY

I hope I did not scare any of you away from seeking men in relationships. Attempting to connect with anyone has its share of obstacles, but a plan and marginal effort make for a better potential outcome. My hope is that these words are the catalyst for multiple conversations with the men you meet, or for those in a relationship, the man you already are attempting to build with. Everyone is their own person, but there are many generalities that hold true. Take the time to ask any man anything from this literary piece. Do not let the open mind that I initially requested at the beginning of this material, close with the closing of these pages. Is this all you need to know about men? Of course it isn't. When you meet someone who is 'worth it', hopefully they are unique in their own way, but familiar to your desires and needs because you were diligent in your fact finding.

I would like to thank you for taking the time to be open and receptive to this material. It is not intended to become a 'How-To' manual, but I trust you will take something away from this that you can incorporate or ponder as you move forward.

Navigating through relationships, regardless of status, can be ever-changing. But the key to all of it is communication (on both sides) and a willingness to understand and accept the information shared. Men and women both have a voice. Hopefully both sides will be heard.

If nothing else ladies, I hope the chapter on Know Thy Self was a bit of an eye opener. As individuals, it is tough to look ourselves in the mirror and be brutally honest without slipping into some level of depression. The balance of self-love with honesty typically has most of us leaning towards self-love. It is easier to preserve our positive psyche by being less honest. I implore you all to be as honest as possible, moving towards new ideas to better embrace what you are doing well, and plans to improve your areas of opportunity. Do these things not in hopes of finding and keeping a man, but for yourself. Consistently doing this will move you towards being the woman a man needs, as opposed to being the woman that needs a man.

Thank you.

ACKNOWLEDGEMENTS

PHOTOS TAKEN AND EDITED BY:

NATURALLY GRACEFUL

PHOTOGRAPHY

~ *~

MATURE CONVERSATIONS ABOUT RELATIONSHIPS

Come join us in our conversations on Facebook

www.ingramcontent.com/pod-product-compliance
Lightning Source LLC
LaVergne TN
LVHW081348060426
835508LV00017B/1482